The month of March, from the illuminated manuscript *Les Trés Riches Heures du duc de Berry*

The Story of a Special Day
Volume 88

March

28

87th day of the year
(88th in leap years)
278 days remaining
until the end of the year.

by Michael Dobson

Timespinner
Press

Table of Contents

Cover: Part of an 1899 promotional poster advertising the Barnum & Bailey Greatest Show on Earth — for the Event of the Day.

Jesse Owens

March 28 Quotations

"Children are the only form of immortality that we can be sure of."

Peter Ustinov, actor and writer, died March 28, 2004

"Growing old's like being increasingly penalized for a crime you haven't committed."

Anthony Powell, writer, died March 28, 2000

"It is not the answer that enlightens, but the question."

Eugène Ionesco, playwright, died March 28, 1994

"When I came back to my native country, after all the stories about Hitler, I couldn't ride in the front of the bus. I had to go to the back door. I couldn't live where I wanted. I wasn't invited to shake hands with Hitler, but I wasn't invited to the White House to shake hands with the President, either."

Jesse Owens, Olympic gold medalist, received a posthumous Congressional Gold Medal, March 28, 1990

"Prejudice is a disease. So is fashion. But I will not wear prejudice."

Lady Gaga (Stefani Germanotta), performance artist, born March 28, 1986

"If a symbol should be discovered in a painting of mine, it was not my intention. It is a result I did not seek. It is something that may be found afterwards, and which can be interpreted according to taste."
Marc Chagall, painter, died March 28, 1985

"I hate war as only a soldier who has lived it can, only as one who has seen its brutality, its stupidity."
Dwight D. Eisenhower, 34th US President,
died March 28, 1969

"The human frame being what it is, heart, body and brain all mixed together, and not contained in separate compartments as they will be no doubt in another million years, a good dinner is of great importance to good talk. One cannot think well, love well, sleep well, if one has not dined well."
Virginia Woolf, writer, died March 28, 1941

"History is much more the product of chaos than of conspiracy."
Zbigniew Brzezinski, US National Security Advisor,
born March 28, 1928

"One has to be able to count, if only so that at fifty one doesn't marry a girl of twenty."
Maxim Gorky (Максим Горький), Russian writer, born March 28, 1869 [O.S. March 16 — see pg. 77]

Virginia Woolf (Photo: George Charles Beresford)

Barnum & Bailey Circus poster featuring the owners,
P. T. Barnum and J. A. Bailey

Barnum and Bailey Merge Their Circuses

On March 28, 1881, the Barnum & Bailey Circus, "The Greatest Show on Earth," was formed from the merger of P. T. Barnum's Great Traveling Museum, Menagerie, Caravan, and Hippodrome with the Cooper and Bailey Circus, owned by James A. Bailey.

Phineas Taylor Barnum (July 5, 1810 — April 7, 1891) described himself thus: "I am a showman by profession...and all the gilding shall make nothing else of me." He operated a small newspaper in Connecticut before moving to New York City in 1835, where he started "Barnum's Grand Scientific and Musical Theater," which established its permanent headquarters in the former Scudder's American Museum at the corner of Broadway and Ann Street in New York. Among its exhibits were a flea circus, a loom run by a dog, Ned the Learned Seal, the Feejee Mermaid, famous conjoined (Siamese) twins Chang and Eng, and trained bears, alongside scientific instruments, modern appliances, and a hat worn by Ulysses S. Grant. When people stayed too long, Barnum famously posted a sign, "This Way to the Egress." Not realizing that "egress" meant "exit," people followed the signs only to find themselves outside.

At a time when the total US population was only 32 million, over 38 million customers paid the 25¢ admission to the museum. The five-story building burned to the ground in 1865, and a second museum built by Barnum burned in 1868 under mysterious circumstances. Financially destroyed by the loss, Barnum retired from the museum business.

It was not until Barnum was 61 years old that he became a circus owner. Delavan, Wisconsin, circus promoters Dan Castello and William Cameron Culp approached Barnum to provide financial backing and lend his name to a new circus they had created. Their main competition was the Cooper and Bailey Circus, famous for owning the first baby elephant ever born in the United States. Barnum tried to buy the elephant from Cooper and Bailey, and when that failed, negotiated a merger between the two circuses on March 28, 1881. The combined Barnum & Bailey Circus, now billing itself as "The Greatest Show on Earth," successfully toured the United States and Europe.

P. T. Barnum died in 1891, and James A. Bailey purchased Barnum's share from his widow.

At the time, circuses traveled from town to town using animal-drawn caravans. Meanwhile, a circus started by the Ringling brothers, a family of seven brothers from Baraboo, Wisconsin, became successful enough that it could begin traveling by train. As a result, they were able to build the largest traveling entertainment company of the time and thus became Barnum & Bailey's chief competitor.

James A. Bailey died in 1906, and the Ringling Brothers bought Barnum & Bailey. Originally, the two circuses operated separately, but eventually the two surviving Ringlings decided to merge the two, forming The Ringling Brothers and Barnum & Bailey Greatest Show on Earth. Over the years, they acquired five more circuses, all of which eventually merged with the main company.

The company's reputation was terribly damaged by the Hartford Circus Fire on July 6, 1944, which was one of the worst fire disasters in US history, killing over a hundred people. Among the attendees that day was future actor Charles Nelson Reilly.

As the circus gave way to other forms of entertainment, Ringling Brothers and Barnum & Bailey Circus suffered. In 1956, it moved from the "big top" tent to indoor arenas. In 1967, the circus was sold again to the Feld brothers, Irvin and Israel, and Judge Roy Mark Hofheinz. In 1971, it was purchased by Mattel, but the Felds bought it back in 1982. Today, Feld Entertainment runs Ringling Brothers and Barnum & Bailey, along with monster truck and other arena-type shows.

Ringling Bros. and Barnum & Bailey Circus train (© James G. Howes, used with permission.)

Japanese tea ceremony, Mizuno Toshikata

March 28 Holidays and Celebrations

Commemoration of Sen no Rikyū (Japan)

Sen no Rikyū (千利休) was a major figure in the history of the Japanese tea ceremony, known as chanoyu (茶の湯). Of the three major "head houses" of the Japanese Way of Tea, the Urasenke (裏千家) school commemorates Sen no Rikyū on March 28 each year; the Omotesenke (表千家) school on March 27.

National Black Forest Cake Day (United States)

In the United States, almost every day of the year is dedicated to a particular food. Sponsored by manufacturers, retailers, farmers, or simply fans, these days are often proclaimed by the President, Congress, state governors, or mayors.

March 28 is National Black Forest Cake Day. Black Forest cake is the English name for the German dessert *Schwarzwälder Kirschtorte*, "Black Forest cherry torte." It consists of layers of chocolate cake interspersed with whipped cream and cherries, decorated with more whipped cream and more cherries (usually black cherries or sometimes sour cherries).

In the German version, *Schwarzwälder Kirschwasser* (a liquor distilled from tart cherries) is a legally required ingredient; the US versions are more often made without liquor. The Black Forest in the cake's name comes from the liquor, not from the forest of the same name.

Serf Liberation Day (Bàiwàn Nóngnú Jiěfàng Jìnìan Rì) (Tibet)

Serf Liberation Day (also referred to as Serfs Emancipation Day) (西藏百萬農奴解放紀念日) was established as an annual holiday to mark the day (March 28, 1959) that the People's Republic of China declared the former Tibetan government illegal, thus (according to China) liberating Tibetans from feudalism and theocracy.

Teacher's Day (Czech Republic and Slovakia)

The nations of Czech Republic and Slovakia honor teachers on March 28 each year, marking the birthday of John Amos Comenius, a Czech-speaking Moravian who was one of the first champions of the idea of universal education. Each year, students nominate teachers who most motivate and inspire them; the winner is crowned *Zlatý Ámos* ("Golden Amos").

Weed Appreciation Day (US)

Weed Appreciation Day (March 28) commemorates garden weeds, not marijuana.

Christian Feast Days

In **Western Christianity,** feast days March 28 include saints Guntram, Priscus, and Pope Sixtus III.

In **Eastern Orthodox Christianity**, it is the commemoration of Saint Hilarion, Saint Stephen the wonderworker, Martyr Eustratius of the Kiev Caves, Saint Hesychios the Theologian, and Apostle Herodion. (These are celebrated on April 10 by "Old Calendarists.)

What Happened on March 28?

37 – Caligula Becomes Emperor of Rome

On March 28, 37, 25-year old Gaius Julius Caesar Germanicus, nicknamed Caligula, or "Little Soldier's Boot," entered the city of Rome in triumph after the death of his great-uncle Tiberus, second emperor of Rome, twelve days earlier.

Although Tiberius had persecuted and killed other members of Caligula's family, he had spared Caligula, naming him joint heir along with his own 13-year old grandson Gemellus. The Roman senate, however awarded the young Caligula sole control of the Empire. Caligula was greatly admired, not just because he was someone other than the hated Tiberius, but because of his youth and beauty. Caligula initially ruled with generosity and kindness.

In October of that year, he fell ill, and on his recovery seemed to have changed greatly. He had Gemellus killed, forced his grandmother to commit suicide, and by 39 was conducting treason trials of senators. In 40, he declared himself a god and mandated worship of himself. He replaced the heads of statues of various gods with his own head. In various accounts, he was supposed to have committed incest with his sisters, turned the palace into a brothel, and appointed his horse, Incitatus, to the Senate — though historians debate whether all of these stories are true.

In 41, after four years as emperor, Caligula was assassinated by officers of his own Praetorian Guard. An attempt to abolish the Principate and return rule of Rome to the Senate failed, and Caligula's uncle Claudius became the fourth Emperor of Rome.

Bust of Caligula, repainted to its original colors. Statues in antiquity were frequently painted. (Photo: Giovanni Dall'Orto)

845 – Sack of Paris

On March 28, 845, a force of about 200 Viking ships sailed up the Seine River to Paris to sack the city and hold it ransom until a large bounty was paid by the crown. After the siege of Paris, the Vikings created a permanent settlement in Normandy.

The Viking leader Rollo (Hrólfr), who was part of the 845 siege, became the first ruler of Normandy after agreeing to acknowledge the Frankish monarch King Charles the Simple. The Dukes of Normandy, his descendants, became the Kings of England following the Norman Conquest in 1066.

1802 – Discovery of Pallas

On March 28, 1802, astronomer Heinrich Wilhelm Olbers discovered Pallas, the second asteroid (after Ceres) to be found. Originally, both Ceres and Pallas were counted as planets, bringing the total number to nine. (Uranus had been discovered in 1781.)

In 1807, two more asteroids were discovered (Juno and Vesta), making 11 planets. With the discovery of more and more of these small objects, they were all dropped from the planet list, and a new term, "asteroid," was used to describe them, dropping the total number of planets back down to seven until the discovery of Neptune in 1846. Today, over 100,000 asteroids have been found.

The reason, by the way, that Pluto was dropped from the planet list in 2006 is similar to the reason that Ceres and Pallas are no longer planets: more and more smaller objects have been discovered in what is now called the Kuiper belt, similar to the asteroid belt but far larger. Over a thousand objects have been discoverd in the Kuiper belt, including the dwarf planet Eris, which is larger than Pluto.

1930 – Constantinople Becomes Istanbul

On March 28, 1930, the Turkish government established the Turkish Postal Service Law, which officially requested that foreigners use Istanbul rather than Constantinople as the name of the city, and began refusing to deliver mail addressed to "Constantinople." At the same time, the city of Angora became Ankara.

The name Istanbul (İstanbul in Turkish, with a dot over the "I"), which simply means "in the city," was in use since well before the Ottoman conquest in 1453, with Constantinople a holdover from the Byzantine era. The original name for the city was Byzantium, changed to Constantinople when it was made the eastern Roman capital in 330.

1939 – Siege of Madrid Ends

After a three year siege by Spanish Nationalist troops commanded by Generalissimo Francisco Franco during the Spanish Civil War, the city of Madrid, loyal to the Second Spanish Republic, fell on March 28, 1939. Nearly 200,000 would be executed or died during imprisonment under the Franco regime, which lasted until Franco's death on November 20, 1975.

1942 – St. Nazaire Raid

On March 28, 1942, the Royal Navy and British commandos launched Operation Chariot to take the heavily defended drydocks in German-occupied St. Nazaire, which would force German warships needing repairs to return to Germany rather than have a safe Atlantic coast refuge.

About 350 Royal Navy sailors and 265 commandos attacked a German defending force of some 5,000. Only 228 returned; the rest were killed or captured. The Germans lost over 360, and the facility was destroyed. The St. Nazaire Raid has been called "the greatest raid of all," with over 89 decorations (including five Victoria Crosses) awarded to the British soldiers and sailors.

Three Mile Island Nuclear Power Plant

1979 – Three Mile Island Incident

The most significant accident in United States commercial nuclear energy took place at the Three Mile Island Nuclear Generating Station, located near Middletown, Pennsylvania, on March 28, 1979. The second of the two units, TMI-2, a pressurized water reactor, experienced a cooling system malfunction that resulted in a partial meltdown of the reactor core, and the release of small amounts of radioactive krypton-85 and iodine-131 gas into the surrounding environment.

The situation was complicated by a combination of poorly designed and ambiguous control room indicators and inadequate training, and triggered a five-day long crisis before the situation was brought under control. No lives were lost as a result of the accident, and follow-up epidemiological studies have shown no increase in cancer near the plant.

Public reaction was influenced by the film *The China Syndrome*, about an accident at a nuclear reactor, which was released twelve days before the Three Mile Island accident took place.

Who Was Born on March 28?

Art and Illustration

Fra Bartolomeo (March 28, 1472 – October 6, 1517)

Fra Bartolomeo (next page) was a painter in Florence during the Italian Renaissance.

Business

Gussie Busch (March 28, 1899 – September 29, 1989)

August "Gussie" Busch was the grandson of brewery founder Adolphus Busch and became president and CEO of Anheuser-Busch in 1946. During his tenure, he build the Anheuser-Busch Companies into the largest brewery in the world. He also owned the St. Louis Cardinals baseball franchise from 1953 to his death in 1989.

Frederick Pabst (March 28, 1836 – January 1, 1904)

German-American brewer Frederick Pabst founded the Pabst Brewing Company in Milwaukee, Wisconsin.

Prophet Isaiah, by Fra Bartolomeo

Government, Law, and Politics

Neil Kinnock (March 28, 1942 –)

Neil Kinnock led the British Labour Party in Parliament from 1983 to 1992, and was the longest-serving Leader of the Opposition in British history never to become Prime Minister.

Zbigniew Brzezinski (March 28, 1928 –)

Zbigniew Brzezinski was United States National Security Advisor to US President Jimmy Carter from 1977 to 1981.

Edmund Muskie (March 28, 1914 – March 26, 1966)

Edmund Muskie was Governor of Maine (1955-1959), a US Senator (1959-1980), the Democratic nominee for Vice-President in 1968, a candidate for the Democratic Presidential nomination in 1972, and US Secretary of State from 1980 to 1981.

Senator Edmund Muskie (left), President Jimmy Carter (right)

Aristide Briand (March 28, 1862 – March 7, 1932)

Eleven-time prime minister of France's Third Republic, Aristide Briand co-won the 1926 Nobel Peace Prize. He is remembered for the Kellogg-Briand Pact (with US Secretary of State Frank B. Kellogg), which unsuccessfully outlawed war.

Thomas Clarkson (March 28, 1760 – September 26, 1846)

English abolitionist Thomas Clarkson established the Society for Effecting the Abolition of the Slave Trade, a powerful lobbying force that helped pass the Slave Trade Act of 1807, which ended the British slave trade.

Samuel Sewall (March 28, 1652 – January 1, 1730)

Samuel Sewall was a judge in the Salem witch trials, and the only magistrate involved who later apologized for his role. He was the official printer of the Massachusetts Bay Colony, and published the first American edition of John Bunyan's *The Pilgrim's Progress*. He wrote *The Selling of Joseph*, the first anti-slavery tract, in 1700.

Letters

Lauren Weisberger (March 28, 1977 –)

Lauren Weisberger wrote the 2003 bestseller *The Devil Wears Prada*, made into a 2006 film starring Meryl Streep and Anne Hathaway.

Mario Vargas Llosa (March 28, 1936 –)

Mario Vargas Llosa won the Nobel Prize in Literature for 2010.

Byrd Baylor (March 28, 1924 –)

Four of Byrd Baylor's children's books have been awarded Caldecott Honors.

A. Bertram Chandler (March 28, 1912 – June 6, 1984)

Merchant marine captain A. Bertram Chandler wrote over 40 novels and 200 short pieces, primarily science fiction. He was noted for his realistic description of life aboard spaceships, which derived from his maritime experience. He won four Ditmar Awards, the Australian equivalent of science fiction's Hugo Award.

Nelson Algren (March 28, 1909 – May 9, 1981)

Algren's 1949 novel *The Man with the Golden Arm* won the National Book Award and was adapted into a 1955 film.

His 1956 novel *A Walk on the Wild Side* contains his famous "three rules of life:" never play cards with a man called Doc. Never eat at a place called Mom's. Never sleep with a woman whose troubles are worse than your own.

Maxim Gorky (March 28, 1868 [O. S. March 16] – June 18, 1936)

Russian author Alexei Peshkov, better known under his pen name Maxim Gorky (Макси́м Го́рький), pioneered the Socialist Realism literary school.

Angry about life under the Russian Empire, he began using the pseudonym Gorky ("bitter"), and in 1898 published his first collection *Essays and Stories* to great popular and critical acclaim.

His involvement with the Marxist social-democratic movement led to a personal friendship with Vladimir Lenin, who sent him on a fund-raising trip to the United States on behalf of the Bolshevik movement.

He wrote his famous novel *The Mother (Мать)* in the Adirondack Mountains. Although he remained close to the Bolsheviks during the Russian Revolution, he began to criticize them in his writing, calling his former friend Lenin "a cold-blooded trickster who spares neither the honor nor the life of the proletariat."

He moved to Italy, where he stayed until financial needs drove him back to the Soviet Union in what the Soviets felt was a major propaganda victory. Although he refrained from criticizing Stalin's government, he was placed under house arrest in 1934. Stalin himself was one of the pallbearers at Gorky's funeral, but there is continued speculation that Gorky was killed by NKVD agents.

Maxim Gorky (right) with Leo Tolstoy, 1900
(Photo: Sofia Andreevna Tolstoy)

Music

Lady Gaga (March 28, 1966 –)

Under her stage name Lady Gaga, Stefani Germanotta's music and performance art has led to five Grammy Awards and 13 Video Music Awards, and was listed by *Forbes* magazine as one of the World's 100 Most Powerful Women and as one of the most influential people in the world by *Time* magazine. Her hits include "Just Dance," "Bad Romance," and "Born This Way."

Lady Gaga

Cheryl "Salt" James (March 28, 1966 –)

Cheryl James was "Salt" in the rap group Salt-n-Pepa.

Reba McEntire (March 28, 1955 –)

Country music artist Reba McEntire is called the "Queen of Country," and has sold more than 80 million records. She starred in her own television sitcom, *Reba*, from 2001 to 2007, and was nominated for a Golden Globe in that role. She holds the record for the most Academy of Country Music Top Female Vocalist awards and for the most American Music Awards for Favorite Country Female Artists.

Thad Jones (March 28, 1923 – August 21, 1986)

Jazz trumpeter Thad Jones began with the Count Basie Orchestra, and formed the Thad Jones/Mel Lewis Orchestra in 1965. In 1985, he became leader of the Count Basie Orchestra on the death of Count Basie.

Jay Livingston (March 28, 1915 – October 17, 2001)

Composer Jay Livingston and his partner Ray Evans won three Academy Awards for Best Original Song for "Buttons and Bows," "Mona Lisa," and "Que Sera, Sera." He is a member of the Songwriters Hall of Fame. His brother Alan created Bozo the Clown and signed Frank Sinatra and the Beatles for Capitol Records.

Rudolf Serkin (March 28, 1903 – May 8, 1991)

Pianist Rudolf Serkin was regarded as one of the great Beethoven interpreters of the 20th century. He received the Presidential Medal of Freedom in 1963, Kennedy Center Honors in 1981, and the National Medal of Arts in 1988.

Jaromír Vejvoda (March 28, 1902 – November 13, 1988)

Czech composer Jaromír Vejvoda wrote the "Beer Barrel Polka."

Paul Whiteman (March 28, 1890 – December 29, 1967)

Bandleader Paul Whiteman (next page)was known as the King of Jazz for his role in popularizing the new musical style. He commissioned George Gershwin's *Rhapsody in Blue* and his arranger Ferde Grofé wrote the *Grand Canyon Suite*. He employed at different times Bix Beiderbecke, Frankie Trumbauer, Joe Venuti, Eddie Lang, Jack Teagarden, Bing Crosby, Paul Robeson, and Billie Holiday. His hits ranged from "Wang Wang Blues" and "Mississippi Mud" to "I'll Build a Stairway to Paradise" and "Parade of the Wooden Soldiers." He was named to the Grammy Hall of Fame in 1998.

Performing Arts

Lacey Turner (March 28, 1988 –)

Lacey Turner has won 33 awards for her role as Stacy Slater on the BBC soap opera EastEnders, and has won more British Soap Awards than any other actor.

Paul Whiteman from the trailer from *Rhapsody in Blue* (1945)

Julia Stiles (March 28, 1981 –)

Julia Stiles began in teen films including 10 *Things I Hate About You*, played Nicky Parsons in the *Bourne* film series, and earned Emmy and Golden Globe nominations for her role in the Showtime series *Dexter*.

Vince Vaughn (March 28, 1970 –)

Vince Vaughn first came to prominence in the 1966 film *Swingers*, and appeared in such films as *Wedding Crashers, Dodgeball: A True Underdog Story, Be Cool*, and many others.

Dianne Wiest (March 28, 1948 –)

Dianne Wiest won two Academy Awards, two Emmy Awards, and a Golden Globe Award. Her notable films include *Hannah and Her Sisters, Parenthood, Edward Scissorhands, Bullets Over Broadway*, and *The Horse Whisperer*.

Ken Howard (March 28, 1944 –)

Ken Howard played Thomas Jefferson in *1776* and the lead role in the television series *The White Shadow*. He was elected president of the Screen Actors Guild in 2009.

Conchata Ferrell (March 28, 1943 –)

Conchata Ferrell came to prominence in the original Broadway cast of *The Hot L Baltimore;* appeared in such films as *Mystic Pizza, Edward Scissorhands*, and E*rin Brockovich;* and on television shows including *The Hot L Baltimore, E/R, L. A. Law,* and *Two and a Half Men.*

Dorothy DeBorba (March 28, 1925 – June 2, 2010)

Child actress Dorothy DeBorba (next page) was a regular in the *Our Gang/Little Rascals* shorts from 1930 to 1933.

Dorothy DeBorba from *School's Out* (1930)

Freddie Bartholomew (March 28, 1924 – January 23, 1992)

Child star Freddie Bartholomew's famous films include *David Copperfield, Captains Courageous* and *Little Lord Fauntleroy.* He was not successful in the transition to adult roles, and became a television producer and executive, producing *The Andy Griffith Show, As The World Turns, The Edge of Night,* and *Search for Tomorrow.*

Dirk Bogarde (March 28, 1921 – May 8, 1999)

English actor Dirk Bogarde's films included *Doctor in the House, A Tale of Two Cities, The Night Porter, Oh! What a Lovely War,* and *A Bridge Too Far.* He was nominated for six Best Actor BAFTA Awards, winning twice, and was made a knight by Queen Elizabeth II in 1992. Later in life, he wrote seven best-selling volumes of memoirs, six novels, and a collection of journalism pieces.

Edward Anhalt (March 28, 1914 – September 3, 2000)

Screenwriter and producer Edward Anhalt, along with his wife Edna, won an Academy Award for the script to 1950's *Panic in the Streets,* and following their divorce won a solo Academy Award for his 1964 adaptation of *Becket.* He also scripted *The Boston Strangler, The Satan Bug, Jeremiah Johnson,* and the ABC miniseries *QB VII.*

Jimmie Dodd (March 28, 1910 – November 10, 1964)

Jimmie Dodd (right) was the MC of the 1950s version of The Mickey Mouse Club and wrote its famous theme song, "The Mickey Mouse Club March."

Irving "Swifty" Lazar (March 28, 1907 – July 13, 1996)

Legendary superagent Swifty Lazar received his nickname from Humphrey Bogart after putting together three major deals for Bogart on the same day.

The Mickey Mouse Club Mousketeers, 1957.
Jimmie Dodd is in the center rear.

His client list included Lauren Bacall, Truman Capote, Cher, Joan Collins, Noël Coward, Cary Grant, Ernest Hemingway, Gene Kelly, Madonna, Walter Matthau, Vladimir Nabokov, Richard Nixon, Cole Porter, and Tennessee Williams.

Pandro S. Berman (March 28, 1905 – July 13, 1996)

Film producer Pandro S. Berman produced Fred Astaire/Ginger Rogers films for RKO, as well as numerous films for MGM. His films received six Academy Award nominations for Best Picture, and Berman himself received the Irving G. Thalberg Memorial Award in 1976.

Charles Starrett (March 28, 1903 – March 22, 1986)

Charles Starrett starred in the *Durango Kid* series of Western movies.

Public Figures

Kate Gosselin (March 28, 1975 –)

Reality TV personality Kate Gosselin came to fame on *Jon & Kate Plus 8*, raising a family of sextuplets and twins.

Herschel Grynszpan (March 28, 1921 – declared dead 1960)

German-born Jewish refugee Herschel Grynszpan assassinated German diplomat Ernst vom Rath on November 7, 1938 in Paris.

The Nazi government used this assassination as the pretext for Kristallnacht, the infamous antisemetic pogrom that began two days later. After the German invasion of France, Grynszpan was taken by the Gestapo and brought to Germany.

For various reasons, he could not be safely tried, and he disappeared while in Nazi custody. He was last known to be alive in early 1944, and was declared officially dead in 1960.

He was the subject of Jonathan Kirsch's *The Short Strange Life of Herschel Grynszpan* and Sir Michael Tippett's oratorio *A Child of Our Time.*

Herschel Grynszpan
(Bundesarchiv, Bild 146-1988-078-08 / CC-BY-SA)

Religion

John Neumann (March 28, 1811– January 5, 1860)

Catholic priest and Bishop of Philadelphia, John Neumann founded the first Catholic diocesan school system in the United States. He was canonized by Pope Paul VI in 1977, becoming the first (and so far only) American male citizen to be made a saint.

Teresa of Ávila (March 28, 1515 – October 4, 1582)

Spanish mystic and nun Teresa of Ávila was canonized in 1622 for her work in reforming the Carmelite Order and for her books *Castillo Interior (The Interior Castle)* and *Camino de Perfección (The Way of Perfection.)*

Teresa of Ávila by Peter Paul Rubens

Science

Alexander Grothendieck (March 28, 1928 –)

Stateless mathematician Alexander Grothendieck is the creator of modern algebraic geometry, which has led to major advances in many areas of pure matheamtics. A long list of mathematical theorems bear his name.

Marlin Perkins (March 28, 1905 – June 14, 1986)

Zoologist Marlin Perkins (right) is best known as the host of the nature show *Mutual of Omaha's Wild Kingdom* from 1963 to 1985.

He was director of Chicago's Lincoln Park Zoo and the St. Louis Zoo, and Sir Edmund Hillary's zoologist on his 1960 Himalayan search for the legendary yeti.

After it was revealed that the Disney film *White Wilderness* had staged a mass suicide of lemmings, journalist Bob McKeown interviewed Marlin Perkins, then in his seventies, and asked him whether he'd ever done anything like that. Perkins asked that the camera be turned off, then punched McKeown in the face.

Sports

Bart Conner (March 28, 1958 –)

Gymnast Bart Conner won an Olympic gold medal on the parallel bars in the 1984 Olympics, and is married to Romanian gymnast and gold medalist Nadia Comăneci.

Ronnie Ray Smith (March 28, 1949 – March 31, 2013)

Sprinter Ronnie Ray Smith won a gold medal in the 1968 Summer Olympics in Mexico City and set a World Junior Record in the 100 meter race.

Rick Barry (March 28, 1944 –)

Basketball small forward Rick Barry played for the San Francisco Warriors, the Oakland Oaks, the Washington Caps, the New York Jets, the Golden State Warriors, and the Houston Rockets in a career that lasted from 1965 to 1980. He was inducted into the Naismith Memorial Basketball Hall of Fame in 1987.

Joey Maxim (March 28, 1922 – June 2, 2001)

Boxer Giuseppe Berardinelli adopted his ring name "Joey Maxim" from the Maxim machine gun because of his rapid-fire left jabs. He was Light Heavyweight Champion of the World from 1950 to 1953. His most famous fight was his 1952 bout with Sugar Ray Robinson, the only time Robinson was stopped in a 201-fight career.

Vic Raschi (March 28, 1919 – October 14, 1988)

Pitcher Vic Raschi played for the New York Yankees, the St. Louis Cardinals, and the Kansas City Athetics in a career that lasted from 1946 to 1955. With the Cardinals, he was responsible for allowing Hank Aaron's first career home run.

Buck Shaw (March 28, 1899 – March 19, 1977)

Football player and coach Buck Shaw was part of Knute Rockne's first unbeaten University of Notre Dame team and was inducted into the College Football Hall of Fame. He was the first Air Force Academy varsity head football coach and coached the San Francisco 49ers and the Philadelphia Eagles.

Tillie Voss (March 28, 1897 – 1975)

During his tenure with the Green Bay Packers, tackle Tillie Voss, along with Frank Hanny of the Chicago Bears, were the first players in league history to be ejected from a game for exchanging punches.

Sepp Herberger (March 28, 1897 – April 28, 1977)

German footballer (soccer) player and manager Josef "Sepp" Herberger is famous as the manager of the underdog 1954 West German national team that won the 1954 FIFA World Cup, known as *Das Wunder von*

Bern ("The Miracle of Bern"), documented in a 2003 German film of the same name.

Martin Sheridan (March 28, 1881 – March 27, 1918)

The New York Times called Martin Sheridan "one of the greatest athletes [the United States] has ever known." He was a five-time Olympic gold medalist (with nine total medals) in the discus throw, the Greek discus, the standing long jump, and the shot put. He died in the 1918 flu pandemic that killed between 50 to 100 million people worldwide.

John Geiger (March 28, 1873 – December 6, 1956)

John Geiger won an Olympic gold medal in men's rowing in the 1900 Paris Olympic Games.

Who Died on March 28?

Art

Marc Chagall (July 6 [O.S. June 24] — March 28, 1985)

Modernist painter Marc Chagall (next page) was noted for painting, book illustration, stained glass, stage design, ceramics, tapestries, and art prints. Picasso said of him, "When Matisse dies, Chagall will be the only painter left who understands what colour really is."

Government

Caspar Weinberger (August 18, 1917 — March 28, 2006)

Caspar Weinberger was the 15th US Secretary of Defense under Ronald Reagan, the 10th US Secretary of Health, Education, and Welfare under Richard Nixon and Gerald Ford, and held a variety of other senior governmental posts. Known by the nickname "Cap the Knife" for his cost cutting initiatives, he nevertheless oversaw a massive defense buildup during his tenure.

He was indicted for his role in selling US missiles to Iran during the Iran-Contra affair against specific Congressional prohibitions, but was pardoned by President George H. W. Bush before he could be put on trial.

I and the Village, Marc Chagall (1911)

Dwight D. Eisenhower (October 14, 1890 — March 28, 1969)

Dwight David Eisenhower was the 34th President of the United States. During World War II, he was Supreme Commander of the Allied Expeditionary Force (SHAEF), in which he planned and carried out Operation Overlord, the invasion of Normandy generally referred to as D-Day.

A West Point graduate, Eisenhower trained tank crews during World War I, and subsequently participated in a famous transcontinental Army convoy that dramatized the poor state of roads in the United States. He was an early and controversial advocate of speed-oriented tank warfare along with George S. Patton, and served as the assistant to several generals, including Douglas MacArthur during his time as Army Chief of Staff and in the Philippines.

His relationship with MacArthur was notoriously rocky. MacArthur habitually referred to Eisenhower as "the best company clerk I ever had." Asked by a reporter in later years if he had known MacArthur, Eisenhower famously replied, "Oh, yes, I studied dramatics under him for twelve years."

Although Eisenhower had never held an active combat command, he became a protégé of Army Chief of Staff George C. Marshall, who was noted for his ability to spot talent, and rose quickly. Eisenhower led Operation Torch in North Africa at the beginning of US military involvement in World War II in Europe. When President Franklin D. Roosevelt decided he could not spare Marshall to command forces in Europe, Marshall chose Eisenhower instead.

Eisenhower served as Military Governor of postwar Germany, as Chief of Staff of the Army (replacing Marshall), as President of Columbia University, and as first Supreme Commander of NATO before running for the Presidency, where his political slogan "I Like Ike" became famous.

As President, Eisenhower championed the Interstate Highway System (based in part on his experiences in the transcontinental Army convoy) and developed the Cold War nuclear strategy.

He was an early political leader in ending segregation and famously sent the Arkansas National Guard and the 101st Airborne Division to desegregate Little Rock (Arkansas) public schools.

From left to right: General Omar Bradley, General Dwight D. Eisenhower, and General George S. Patton, during the Battle of the Bulge, 1944

Ivan the Terrible (August 25, 1530 — March 28 [O.S. March 18], 1584)

Grand Prince of Moscow Ivan IV Vasilyevich (next page) was crowned the first Tsar of All the Russias in 1547 after conquering the lands of Kazan, Astrakhan, and Siberia, turning the small state of Moscow into a great empire. The "Terrible" title in Russian means "inspiring fear or terror" or being formidable and dangerous. Although intelligent and devout, he suffered from mental illness and fits of rage. During one such rage, he beat his son and heir to death. (For an explanation of "O. S.," see page 77.)

Letters

Anthony Powell (December 21, 1905 — March 28, 2000)

Known for his twelve-volume *A Dance to the Music of Time,* Anthony Powell was named by the London Times as one of the 50 greatest British writers since 1945.

Eugène Ionesco (November 26, 1909 — March 28, 1994)

Theatre of the Absurd playwright Eugène Ionesco's best known play is 1959's *Rhinocéros,* in which the leading character watches as his friends, one by one, turn into rhinoceroses. It is seen as a response to the rise of Communism, Fascism, and Nazism and a commentary on conformity and mass movements.

Ivan the Terrible by Viktor M. Vasnetsov, 1897

Virginia Woolf (January 25, 1882 — March 28, 1941)

Virginia Woolf (page 5) was a central figure in the Bloomsbury Group of intellectuals and is considered one of the foremost modernist authors of the twentieth century. Her best-known works include *Mrs Dalloway, To the Lighthouse, Orlando,* and *A Room of One's Own.*

Music

Earl Scruggs (January 6, 1924 — March 28, 2012)

Bluegrass and country banjo player Earl Scruggs popularized the three-finger banjo-picking "Scruggs style." He played for many years with Bill Monroe's Blue Grass Boys and later partnered with guitarist Lester Flatt to form Flatt and Scruggs and the Foggy Mountain Boys.

His most famous mainstream hit is "The Ballad of Jed Clampett," the theme song for the TV sitcom *The Beverly Hillbillies.* He is also known for his recordings of the Grammy-winning "Foggy Mountain Breakdown" and "Dueling Banjos."

He received a Grammy Lifetime Achievement Award, the National Medal of Arts, and was an inaugural inductee into the International Bluegrass Hall of Fame and a member (with Flatt) of the Country Music Hall of Fame.

Maurice Jarre (September 13, 1924 — March 28, 2009)

Composer Maurice Jarre is best known for his film scores. He received nine Academy Award nominations, winning three for Best Original Score for *Lawrence of Arabia, Doctor Zhivago,* and *A Passage to India.*

Rusty Draper (January 25, 1923 — March 28, 2003)

Country and pop singer Rusty Draper had a gold record with his 1953 hit "Gambler's Guitar," and charted with "Seventeen," "The Shifting, Whispering Sands," and "Are You Satisfied?" He hosted the 1966 NBC daytime series *Swingin' Country.*

Maria von Trapp (January 26, 1905 — March 28, 1987)

Schoolteacher and prospective nun Maria Kutschera was asked to teach one of the children of widowed Austrian naval officer Captain Georg Johannes von Trapp, whose wife had died from scarlet fever. She married Trapp in 1927. In 1935, the bank the Trapps used failed, leaving the family destitute, and they began singing in concerts to make money. They fled Europe after the rise of Naziism, settled in the United States, and continued to tour.

Maria's 1949 book *The Story of the Trapp Family Singers* became a best seller, resulting in two German-language films (*The Trapp Family* and *The Trapp Family in America*) before being adapted into the Rodgers and Hammerstein play and film *The Sound of Music*. Maria and two of her daughters can be seen briefly in the film walking past an archway during the song "I Have Confidence."

Dorothy Fields (July 15, 1905 — March 28, 1974)

Dorothy Fields wrote more than 400 songs for Broadway musicals and films, including "I Can't Give You Anything But Love," "On the Sunny Side of the Street," "The Way You Look Tonight," and many others, working with collaborators such as Jerome Kern, Irving Berlin, Jimmy McHugh, and Arthur Schwartz.

Arthur "Big Boy" Crudup (August 24, 1905 — March 28, 1974)

Delta blues singer, songwriter, and guitarist Arthur Crudup's hits include "That's All Right," "My Baby Left Me," and "So Glad You're Mine," all of which were later covered by Elvis Presley.

W. C. Handy (November 16, 1873 — March 28, 1958)

Influential American songwriter W. C. Handy is known as the "Father of the Blues." His many compositions include "Memphis Blues," "Yellow Dog Blues," "Saint Louis Blues," "Beale Street Blues," and the "Ole Miss Rag." The 1958 film *St. Louis Blues* was about him, with Nat "King" Cole playing Handy.

Sergei Rachmaninoff (April 1 [O.S. March 20], 1881 — March 28, 1943)

Composer Sergei Rachmaninoff best known compositions include *Rhapsody on a Theme of Paganini,* his one-act opera *Aleko,* his *Piano Concerto No. 2 in C minor, Op. 18,* and others. He left Russia after the 1917 Russian Revolution and emigrated to the United States, where he was a successful concert pianist and conductor. (For an explanation of "O.S.," see page 77.)

Modest Mussorgsky (March 21 [O.S. March 9], 1881 — March 28 [O.S. March 16], 1881)

Mussorgsky (right, painting by Ilya Repin) is one of the best known Russian composers of the romantic period. Among his well known works are the opera *Boris Godunov,* the tone poem *Night on Bald Mountain,* and the piano suite *Pictures at an Exhibition.*

Performing Arts

June Havoc (November 8, 1912 — March 28, 2010)

June Havoc began as a vaudeville child actress known as "Baby June" and "Dainty June" before leaving her mother's company and beginning a Broadway and film career. Her last major role was in the daytime drama *General Hospital*. Her sister Louise, later known as burlesque performer Gypsy Rose Lee, wrote a memoir of those early days, which became the Broadway hit and movie *Gypsy*. Havoc herself wrote two memoirs and a play that briefly ran on Broadway.

Peter Ustinov (April 16, 1921 — March 28, 2004)

English actor, writer, and dramatist Sir Peter Ustinov's many films include *We're No Angels*, *Quo Vadis*, *Spartacus*, *Billy Budd*, and *Topkapi*. He was well known for playing Agatha Christie's character Hercule Poirot in six films, beginning with *Death on the Nile*. He won two Academy Awards for Best Supporting Actor. He also directed several operas, wrote over 30 books, served as a Goodwill Ambassador for UNICEF, and was a highly sought-after talk show guest.

Hugh O'Connor (April 7, 1962 — March 28, 1995)

Hugh O'Connor played Detective Lonnie Jamison on the TV series *In The Heat of the Night* alongside his father Carroll O'Connor. He committed suicide in 1995 after a long struggle with drugs.

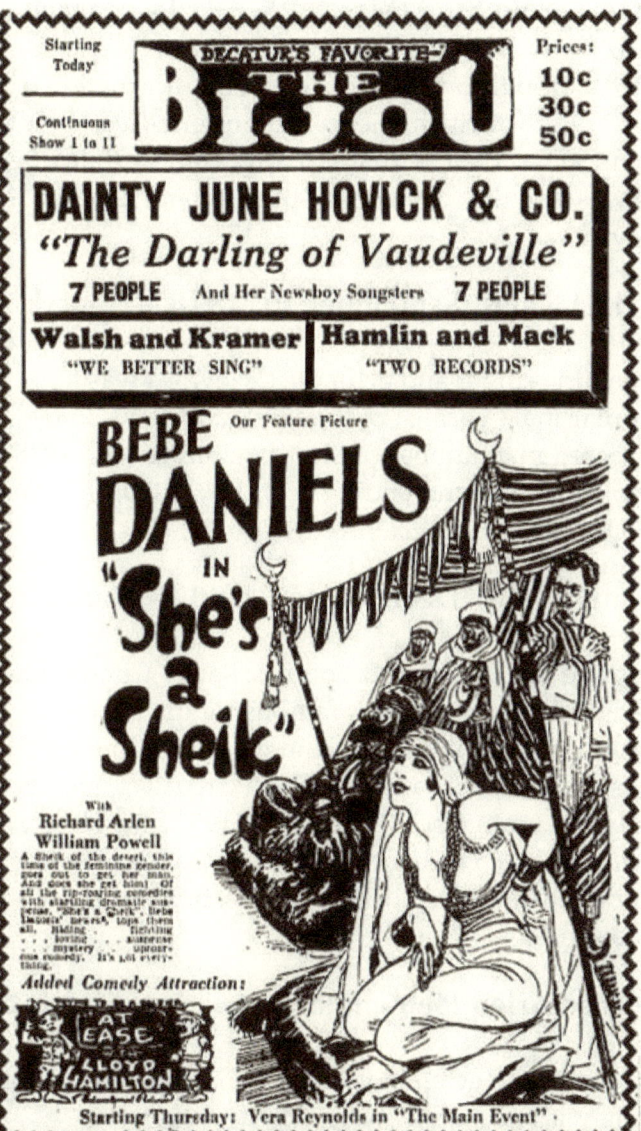

Advertisement for a vaudeville show featuring "Dainty June and her Newsboy Songsters," 1927

Patrick Troughton (March 25, 1920 — March 28, 1987)

Patrick Troughton played the second incarnation of the Doctor in the British science fiction series *Doctor Who* from 1966 to 1969, with guest appearances thereafter. He was also the first actor to play Robin Hood on television.

Dick Haymes (September 13, 1918 — March 28, 1980)

Argentine singer and actor Dick Haymes was a popular male vocalist of the 1940s and 1950s and appeared in a number of films beginning with 1938's *Dramatic School* and ending with 1976's *Won Ton Ton, the Dog Who Saved Hollywood.*

Emmett Kelly (December 9, 1898 — March 28, 1979)

Ringling Brothers and Barnum & Bailey Circus clown Emmett Kelly (right) was famous for his hobo character "Weary Willie," who would try to sweep up the spotlight circle at the end of a circus act. He played his character in Cecil B. DeMille's 1952 film *The Greatest Show on Earth.* During the Hartford Circus Fire, he attempted to extinguish the flames, but was not successful.

Richard Arlen (September 1, 1899 — March 28, 1976)

Richard Arlen acted in more than one hundred films, along with numerous television appearances.

Emmett Kelly (Photo: Joseph Steinmetz)

Jack Hoxie (January 11, 1885 — March 28, 1965)

Rodeo performer and actor Jack Hoxie is known for his silent film era Westerns.

Movie poster for the 1919 film *Lightning Bryce*, Jack Hoxie's first starring role

Sports

Jim Thorpe (May 28, 1888 — March 28, 1953)

Voted the Greatest Athlete of the Twentieth Century, Jim Thorpe won Olympic gold medals in pentathlon and decathlon, and played collegiate and professional football, professional basketball, and professional baseball. Of combined Native American and European ancestry, he was known in the Sauk language as Wa-Tho-Huk, or "Bright Path.

Jim Thorpe

Marcus Hurley (December 22, 1883 — March 28, 1941)

American cyclist Marcus Hurley won four Olympic gold medals and a bronze medal in the 1904 St. Louis Summer Olympic Games.

März (March), by Hans Thoma

The Month of March

"Up from the sea, the wild north wind is blowing
Under the sky's gray arch;
Smiling I watch the shaken elm boughs, knowing
It is the wind of March."

— "March," John Greenleaf Whittier

In ancient Rome, March was the first month of the year.
As the first month of spring, in the Mediterranean
climate it marked the beginning of the military
campaign season. That's why March (Martius) is
named in honor of Mars, the Roman god of war.

Although the first month of the year was moved
back to January sometime during the transition of
Rome from a kingdom to a republic (historians differ),
March was the first month of the year in Russia until
the end of the 15th Century, and is the first month of
the year in many other cultures and religions.

In the northern hemisphere, March 1 marks the
beginning of meteorological spring. In the southern
hemisphere, March is the equivalent of September,
making southern hemisphere March the beginning of
autumn.

March is one of the seven months that have 31 days in it. March starts on the same day of the week as November every year, and except for leap years starts on the same day as February. March starts on the same day of the week as the previous June except for leap years, and in leap years starts on the same day as the previous September and December.

March in Other Cultures

The month of March has different names in different languages. Some nations use calendars other than the Gregorian, and their months may overlap with March.

- Arabic (Egypt, Sudan, Yemen): مارس (Māris)
- Chinese and Japanese: 三月
- Croatian: Ožujak
- Czech: Březen
- Finnish: Maaliskuu (earthy month).
- Greek: Μάρτιος
- Hebrew: מרץ
- Hindi: मार्च
- Korean: 3 월에 (3 wol-e)
- Old English: Hreþmōnaþ
- Polish: Marzec
- Russian: март
- Slovene: Sušec
- Ukranian: березень (birch tree)
- Vietnamese: 腩罷 (tháng ba)

March Superstitions

"Beware the Ides of March (March 15)!"

"March comes in like a lion and goes out like a lamb."

"April borrowed from March three days, and they were ill."

The first three days of March are unlucky "blind days." If rain falls on these days, farmers will have poor harvests.

Children born on Easter Day will be fortunate; children born on Good Friday are doomed to be unlucky.

"If Our Lord falls in Our Lady's lap/England will meet with a great mishap." (If Good Friday or Easter fall on Lady Day, March 25, the Feast of the Annunciation of Our Lady, national misfortune will befall.)

Clothes washed on Good Friday will never come clean.

Children should not climb trees on Good Friday.

Bread baked on Good Friday will never go moldy; eggs laid on Good Friday will no spoil.

Marriages that take place during Lent will have trouble.

"Married when March winds shrill and roar/Your home will be on a distant shore."

Good days to be married in March are March 3, 5, 13, 20, and 23. Which day? "Monday for wealth, Tuesday for health, Wednesday the best day of all, Thursday for losses, Friday for crosses, Saturday for no luck at all."

March Symbols

Birthstone
Aquamarine (left) and bloodstone, both representing faithfulness, courage, and friendship.

Birth Flowers
Daffodils (right), symbolizing rebirth and new beginning. Daffodils are also the 10th wedding anniversary flower.

March Events

Honorary Months

Presidents, Congresses, and nations around the world issue proclamations recognizing particular months to honor certain causes. These events generally fall in March. (All US unless otherwise noted.)

- American Red Cross Month
- Child Life Month
- Fire Prevention Month (The Philippines)
- Irish-American Heritage Month
- Colorectal Cancer Awareness Month
- National Caffeine Awareness Month
- National Celery Month
- National Cheerleading Safety Month
- National Flour Month
- National Frozen Food Month
- National Noodle Month
- National Nutrition Month
- National Peanut Month
- National Sauce Month
- Women's History Month (celebrated in Canada during October)

Women's Suffrage Demonstration 1917

"March Madness" (United States)

The NCAA Men's Division I Basketball Championship, popularly known as "March Madness" or the "Big Dance," is a single-elimination tournament to establish the champion college basketball team.

Moveable and Multi-Day Events

Some events take place over a specific week or time period. Start and finish dates may vary from year to year. Some events occur on different days each year (such as "fourth Saturday of a month").

Birkat Hachama (ברכת החמה) (Judaism)

According to the Talmud, the Sun was created at the vernal equinox position at the beginning of the Jewish month of Nisan, established by tradition as March 25 on the Julian calendar (see "On Names and Dates").

The Birkat Hachama, "Blessing of the Sun" is recited when the vernal equinox occurs at sundown on a Tuesday, which happens every 28 years. When the Julian calendar gave way to the Gregorian calendar in 1582, the date shifted forward, and continues to shift slowly forward by approximately a day per century.

Birkat Hachama took place on April 8, 2009 (14 Nisan 5769), and will occur next on April 8, 2037 (23 Nisan 5797).

Birkat Hachama at the Western Wall, 2009

Earth Hour (International)

On the last Saturday of March each year, households and business are urged to turn off all non-essential lights for one hour between 8:30 pm to 9:30 pm on each person's local time to raise awareness of the need to take action on climate change.

Meat-Free Week (Australia)

Meat-Free Week, the last week in March, promotes vegetarianism.

National Cleaning Week (US)

National Cleaning Week, the last week of March, reminds us to start our spring cleaning.

Pediatric Nurse Practitioner Week (US)

Pediatric Nurse Practitioner Week is celebrated during the last week of March.

Seward's Day (Alaska)

Seward's Day, celebrated on the last Monday in March, commemorates the signing of the Alaska Purchase Treaty on March 30, 1867.

Easter Season

The Christian holiday of Easter in Western Christianity is held on the first Sunday after the Paschal Full Moon following the March equinox, which is officially set at March 21 by church reckoning. Easter itself can therefore occur as early as March 22 and as late as April 25, but occurs most often in April. In Eastern Christianity, which uses the Julian calendar, Easter occurs between April 4 and May 8. This also sets the date for the various events that lead up to Easter, most importantly the events of Holy Week. (For an explanation of Julian and Gregorian dates, see "On Names and Dates.")

Passion Sunday

The fifth Sunday of the Christian season of Lent is known as Passion Sunday in various Protestant denominations and by some traditionalist Catholics. Sometimes, the sixth Sunday of Lent is referred to as Passion Sunday, but it is more commonly known as Palm Sunday. Passion Sunday starts the two-week Passiontide, which ends on Holy Saturday, the day before Easter, commemorating the day that Jesus's body was laid in the tomb. The fifth Sunday of Lent can occur as early as March 8 (though the next time it will be that early is in 2285 CE), and as late as April 11.

Palm Sunday

The moveable feast of Palm Sunday commemorates the triumphant entry of Jesus into Jerusalem, an event mentioned in all four gospels. In many Christian churches, palm leaves are distributed to the worshippers. The earliest date for Palm Sunday is March 15, and the latest is April 18.

Maundy Thursday

The Thursday before Easter is Maundy Thursday, when the Last Supper took place. Because of its relation to Easter, the earliest day it can occur is March 19, and the latest it can occur is April 22.

Good Friday

Good Friday, observed during Holy Week on the Friday preceding Easter Sunday, commemorates the crucifixion of Jesus and his death at Calvary. Because of its relation to Easter, the earliest day it can occur is March 20, and the latest it can occur is April 23.

Holy Saturday

Sometimes called Easter Eve or Black Saturday, Holy Saturday commemorates the day in which Jesus's body lay in the tomb. Some mistakenly refer to this day as "Easter Saturday," but that properly describes the Saturday following Easter, the last day of Easter Week. The earliest it can occur is March 21, and the latest it can occur is April 24.

La crucifixion by El Greco

Easter

Easter celebrates the resurrection of Jesus Christ on the third day after his crucifixion. In the liturgical calendar, Easter follows the season of Lent, and begins the period known as Eastertide, which ends on Pentecost Sunday. Easter is observed religiously in a morning service. In the U.S., it's also common to decorate Easter eggs and make Easter baskets of eggs and candy, often with the Easter bunny as a symbol. The White House traditionally hosts an egg hunt, and many communities have Easter parades. Easter customs around the world include bonfires (Cyprus, western Sweden), men spanking women with a ceremonial whip (Czech Republic and Slovakia), egg fighting (Bulgaria), cross-country skiing and reading murder mysteries (Norway), and children dressed as witches collecting candy door-to-door (other Nordic countries).

Easter Eggs

Easter Monday

In some Roman Catholic and Eastern Orthodox
cultures, the Monday after Easter is celebrated as a
holiday. It is also known as Egg Nyte, featuring egg
rolling competitions and dousing other people with
water that had been blessed with holy water the
previous day at mass. Easter Monday is also celebrated
as Family Day in South Africa. In Guyana, people fly
kites that were made on Holy Saturday. In Portugal, it
is known as the Anjo (Ivy) Festival, in which people
picnic in the countryside.

Śmigus-Dyngus (Poland, Hungary, Czech Republic, Slovakia)

The Monday after Easter in Poland and in the Polish
diaspora is known as Śmigus-Dyngus, or simply
Dyngus Day in the US. Boys throw water over girls
they like and spank them with pussy willows. Girls
avoid getting wet by giving boys "ransoms" of painted
eggs.

Easter Week (Western Christianity), Bright Week (Eastern Christianity)

The period from Easter Sunday to the following
Saturday is known as Easter Week. In both Western
and Eastern Christianity (where it's known as Bright
Week), the resurrection continues to be celebrated in
church services. Easter Tuesday is a public holiday in
the Australian state of Tasmania.

The Month of March, from the *Brevarium Grimani*

March Zodiac Signs

From the perspective of someone on Earth, the Sun appears to move through the sky throughout the year, along a path astronomers call the ecliptic plane. The ecliptic plane is divided into twelve constellations, known as the zodiac, based on traditionally observed patterns of stars. On your birthday, you can't see your constellation, because it's in the daytime sky.

The zodiac was first developed by Babylonian astronomers about 2,500 years ago. Because they were unaware that the Earth wobbles like a spinning top (known as *precession*), they didn't make allowance for the fact that the Sun's path through the zodiac changes over time.

That means there are now two sets of dates for your birth sign. The *tropical* dates are the original Babylonian dates; the *sidereal* dates tell you where the Sun actually appears as it moves along its annual path.

For March 28, the tropical sign is **Aries**, and the sidereal sign is **Pisces**.

Pisces

Tropical February 20 to March 20
Sidereal March 15 to April 14

In the Roman legend of Venus and her son Cupid, they escaped the clutches of Typhon, known as the "father of all monsters," by transforming into fish and tying themselves together with rope. That's why the name Pisces is plural for fish. The constellation appears as a somewhat ragged "V" shape, representing the rope, with the "fish" located at the two rope ends.

In astrology, Pisces is a water sign, compatible with the other water signs Cancer and Scorpio, as well as with the earth signs Taurus, Virgo, and Capricorn. Pisceans are supposed to be imaginative, compassionate, unworldly, secretive, and escapist.

Aries

Tropical March 21 to April 19
Sidereal April 15 to May 15

In Greek mythology, Aries is a ram with golden wings and golden wool who rescued the twins Phrixus and Helle from certain death. Although Helle died in the rescue attempt, the grateful Phrixus sacrificed the ram to Zeus. The golden fleece from the sacrificed ram played a prominent part in the later myth of Jason and the Argonauts.

In astrology, Aries, a fire sign, is compatible with the other fire signs of Gemini, Leo, and Sagittarius, and to a lesser extent with air signs Scorpio and Libra. Arians are supposed to be adventurous, enthusiastic, quick-tempered, and impulsive.

Illustration by Edward Penfield

What Day of the Week is March 28?

On what day of the week does March 28 fall?

Surprisingly, this isn't an easy question. Because the calendar year is 365 days long (366 in leap years), it doesn't divide evenly by the seven days of the week.

Also, the Earth goes around the Sun in about 365-1/4 days, so a calendar tends to drift over time. That's why the same date falls on different weekdays in different years.

This is made even more complicated by a change in calendars that took place in 1582. Our modern calendar has its roots in ancient Rome, in a calendar reform conducted by Julius Caesar. Caesar commissioned mathematicians to attack the problem, and they came up with the idea of leap years, and thus standardized the calendar for centuries to come. This was called the Julian calendar.

Over time, however, the small errors in Caesar's calculation compounded. That's why Pope Gregory XIII commissioned the Gregorian calendar, used in most of the world today. Some countries converted in 1582, when the calendar was first developed; some converted later; other still haven't changed.

Gregorian and Julian aren't the only types of calendars. The Hebrew year, the Islamic year, and many other calendars are used in different parts of the world and among different people.

You can convert Gregorian dates to other calendars, including the Hebrew calendar, the Islamic calendar, and even the Mayan calendar by visiting the Fourmilab Calendar Converter at http://www.fourmilab.ch/documents/calendar/.

Chinese calendar systems are quite complex and have changed several times; a full discussion is far beyond the scope of this book. If you're interested, you can find information here: http://www.hermetic.ch/cal_stud/chinese_cal.htm.

A 50-year brass perpetual calendar.

On Names and Dates

Historians use "CE" (Common Era) and "BCE" (Before the Common Era) instead of the more common "AD" (Anno Domini, or Year of Our Lord) and "BC" (Before Christ), reflecting the fact that the year-numbering system established by the Gregorian calendar is used throughout the world in many countries not culturally Christian.

The CE/BCE designation dates back to at least 1708, and has been adopted as a standard by the United Nations and the Universal Postal Union. Because this series of books covers events and people of all nations and cultures, we use the CE/BCE terms.

The abbreviation "O.S." ("Old Style") on some dates refers to the fact that the Russian Empire did not switch from the Julian to the Gregorian calendar at the same time as the rest of Europe, and therefore some figures and events have two dates.

Also, in the Julian calendar in England in the 16th century, the year began on March 25 rather than January 1. To avoid confusion with Gregorian dates, dates between January and March were often written using both years.

People and events whose original names are not in the Western alphabet have their native names (where possible) in the appropriate script shown in parenthesis. If you are using an e-reader to access an electronic version of this book, all characters don't always display on all devices.

Cartoon by John T. McCutcheon

Copyright, Credit, and Contact

Follow Us

Our blog Dobson's Improbable History (http://improbhistory.blogspot.com) features short articles on events and people associated with each day, and updates several times each week.

You can also get a daily "What Happened In History" message and all the latest Timespinner Press news by following us on Facebook at https://www.facebook.com/TimespinnerPress. Our Twitter feed @SidewiseThinker links you to all our News of the Day.

Contact Us

Find an error or a format problem? Want information about the series, about us, or about when the volume for your special day might be available? Please email us at editor@timespinnerpress.com. (We also take requests if your special day isn't yet complete. Please give us at least six weeks' notice if possible.)

Sources

We owe a great debt to Wikipedia, which is our first stop for research. We attempt to make independent confirmation of all important dates and facts through a variety of other sources. Other sources we frequently use include the Library of Congress; "on this day" listings from *Encyclopedia Britannica*, the New York *Times*, and the BBC; and, of course, the always essential Google.

All art and photographs are either in the public domain, used under a Creative Commons license, or with a "fair use" justification, and most frequently come from Wikimedia Commons and the Library of Congress Prints and Photographs Division.

Attribution is provided where possible, or as requested by the copyright owner, or when there is particular historical significance, listed below. For information about any particular illustration or photograph, please contact us.

Credits

- The cover is from an 1899 poster advertising the Barnum & Bailey Greatest Show on Earth. It was originally copyright © Strobridge Litho Co., but is in the public domain because its copyright has expired. The original is in the collection of the Library of Congress Prints and Photographs Division.

- The illustration of the month of March is from the French Gothic illuminated manuscript *Les Très Riches Heures du duc de Berry* by the Limbourg Brothers, Jean Colombe, and an intermediate painter whose name is lost to history. It is in the public domain because its copyright has expired.

- The 1936 photograph of Jesse Owens at the Berlin Olympics is in the public domain because its copyright has expired and the author is anonymous.

- The 1902 photograph of Virginia Woolf was taken by George Charles Beresford. It is in the public domain because its copyright has expired.

- The 1897 Barnum & Bailey Circus poster featuring P. T. Barnum and J. A. Bailey was originally copyright © Strobridge Litho Co., but is in the public domain because its copyright has expired. The original is in the collection of the Library of Congress Prints and Photographs Division.

- The photograph of the Ringling Bros. and Barnum & Bailey Circus train in Safety Harbor, Florida, is copyright © James G. Howes 1992. The copyright holder of this file, James G. Howes, allows anyone to use it for any purpose, provided that the copyright holder is properly attributed. Redistribution, derivative work, commercial use, and all other use is permitted.

- The 19th century woodblock print of a Japanese tea ceremony is by Mizuno Toshikata. It is in the public domain because its copyright has expired.

- The photograph of the bust of Caligula with its original colors restored was taken in 2006 by Giovanni Dall'Orto, who owns the copyright. The copyright holder allows anyone to use it for any purpose, provided that the copyright holder is properly attributed. Redistribution, derivative work, commercial use, and all other use is permitted. The bust itself is in the Istanbul Archaeological Museum, but was on loan to the Glyptotek in Munich, Germany, when this photograph was taken. The photograph has been cropped for its use in this book.

- The photograph of the Three Mile Island nuclear power plant is in the public domain because it was taken by an employee of the United States government as part of that person's official duties; the name of the photographer is unknown. The image is from the Centers for Disease Control and Prevention's Public Health Image Library.

- The circa 1516 painting of the Prophet Isaiah by Fra Bartolomeo can be found in the Galleria dell'Acccademia in Florence. The work is in the public domain because its copyright has expired.

- The 1977 photograph of Senator Edmund Muskie and President Jimmy Carter was taken by a White House staff photographer, and is in the public domain as a work of the US Federal government. It is in the collection of the Jimmy Carter Library, National Archives and Records Administration.

- The photograph of Maxim Gorky and Leo Tolstoy was taken by Tolstoy's wife Sofia in 1900. It is in the public domain because its copyright has expired.

- The photograph of Lady Gaga was taken by T. J. Sengel in 2011, and is used here under CC-BY-SA 2.0.

- The screenshot of Paul Whiteman from the trailer from the 1945 film *Rhapsody in Blue* is in the public domain because it was published in the United States between 1923 and 1977 without a copyright notice.

- The photograph of Dorothy DeBorba from the *Our Gang* feature *School's Out* is in the public domain because it was first published in the United States between 1923 and 1963, and although there may or may not have been a copyright notice, the copyright was not renewed.

- The 1956 photograph of the Mickey Mouse Club Mouseketeers is in the public domain because it was first published in the United States between 1923 and 1963, and although there may or may not have been a copyright notice, the copyright was not renewed.

- The 1938 photograph of Herschel Grynszpan is from the German Federal Archives and used here under CC-BY-SA 3.0 Germany.

- The 1615 painting of Teresa of Ávila is by Peter Paul Rubens, and can be found in the collection of the Kunsthistorisches Museum in Vienna, Austria. The photograph was taken in 2005 by David Monniaux and is used here under CC-BY-SA 3.0. The painting itself is in the public domain because its copyright has expired.

- The photograph of Marlin Perkins from *Wild Kingdom* is in the public domain because it was published in the United States between 1923 and 1977 without a copyright notice.

- The 1911 painting "I and the Village" by Marc Chagall is in the public domain in the United States because its copyright has expired. The original is in the collection of New York's Museum of Modern Art.

- The photograph of Omar Bradley, Dwight Eisenhower, and George Patton at the Battle of the Bulge is in the public domain as a work created by a soldier or employee of the US federal government. The photographer is unknown.

- The detail from the 1897 portrait of Tsar Ivan the Terrible by Viktor M. Vasnetsov is in the public domain because its copyright has expired. It has been cropped for its appearance in this book.

- The 1881 painting of Modest Mussorgsky by Ilya Repin is in the public domain because its copyright has expired.

- The advertisement for the vaudeville show featuring "Dainty June" appeared in the November 13, 1927 issue of the *Decatur (Illinois) Review*. It is in the public domain because it was first published in the United States between 1923 and 1977 without a copyright notice.

- The photograph of Emmett Kelly in a bubble bath was taken by Joseph Janney Steinmetz, a well known commercial photographer, as a favor to Kelly, who wanted the image for his Christmas card. The image is in the State Library and Archives of Florida, and no known copyright restrictions exist on the use of this image.

- The movie poster for the 1919 film *Lightning Bryce* is in the public domain because its copyright has expired.

- The Goudey Sport Kings football card of Jim Thorpe is in the public domain because it was published between 1923 and 1963 and its copyright, if any, was not renewed.

- The painting März (March) is from the calendar book *Festkalender* by Hans Thoma. It is in the pubic domain because its copyright has expired.

Michael Dobson

- The photograph of aquamarine has been released into the public domain.

- The photograph of daffodils is by "Myrabella," and is licensed under CC-BY-SA 3.0.

- The 1917 Women's Suffrage demonstration comes from the Library of Congress, Prints and Photographs Division, LC-USZ62-31799 DLC, and is in the public domain because its copyright has expired.

- The 2009 photograph of Birkat Hachama at the Western Wall is by "Ingo," and is used here under CC-BY-SA 3.0.

- The painting *La Crucifixión* by El Greco is located in the Museo del Prado. It is in the public domain because its copyright has expired.

- The photograph of Czechoslovakian Easter eggs was taken by Jan Kameníček, who has released the image into the public domain.

- The painting *März*, from the Flemish *Brevarium Grimani*, is by Gerard Horenbout and Alexander and Simon Bening. It was first published around 1510. It is in the public domain because its copyright has expired. The original is in the Biblioteca Marciana.

- The 1906 automobile calendar is by Edward Penfield, and is in the collection of the Library of Congress Prints and Photographs Division. It is in the public domain because its copyright has expired.

- The 50-year perpetual calendar photograph is in the public domain.

- The cartoon by John T. McCutcheon is from his 1905 collection *The Mysterious Stranger and Other Cartoons by John T. McCutcheon*. It is in the public domain because its copyright has expired.

License Description and Terms

Aside from material purely in the public domain, photographs and other material in this book are used under specific licenses permitting free use, usually with an attribution requirement. For full text and terms of these licenses, click or enter the appropriate links below. If you believe there is an error in the copyright status or attribution of any of these images, please email us.

- Creative Commons Attribution 2.0 Generic (CC-BY 2.0): http://creativecommons.org/licenses/by/2.0/deed.en
- Creative Commons Attribution-Share Alike 3.0 Generic (CC-BY-SA 3.0): http://creativecommons.org/licenses/by-sa/3.0/
- Creative Commons Attribution-Share Alike 2.5 Generic (CC-BY-SA 2.5): http://creativecommons.org/licenses/by-sa/2.5/deed.en
- Creative Commons Attribution-Share Alike 2.0 Generic (CC-BY-SA 2.0): http://creativecommons.org/licenses/by/2.0/deed.en
- Creative Commons Attribution-Share Alike 1.0 Generic (CC-BY-SA 1.0): http://creativecommons.org/licenses/by-sa/1.0/deed.en
- CC0 1.0 Universal (CC0 1.0) Public Domain Dedication (CC0 1.0) http://creativecommons.org/publicdomain/zero/1.0/deed.en
- GNU Free Documentation License (GFDL): http://en.wikipedia.org/wiki/Wikipedia:Text_of_the_GNU_Free_Documentation_License

Timespinner
Press